Contents

Introduction

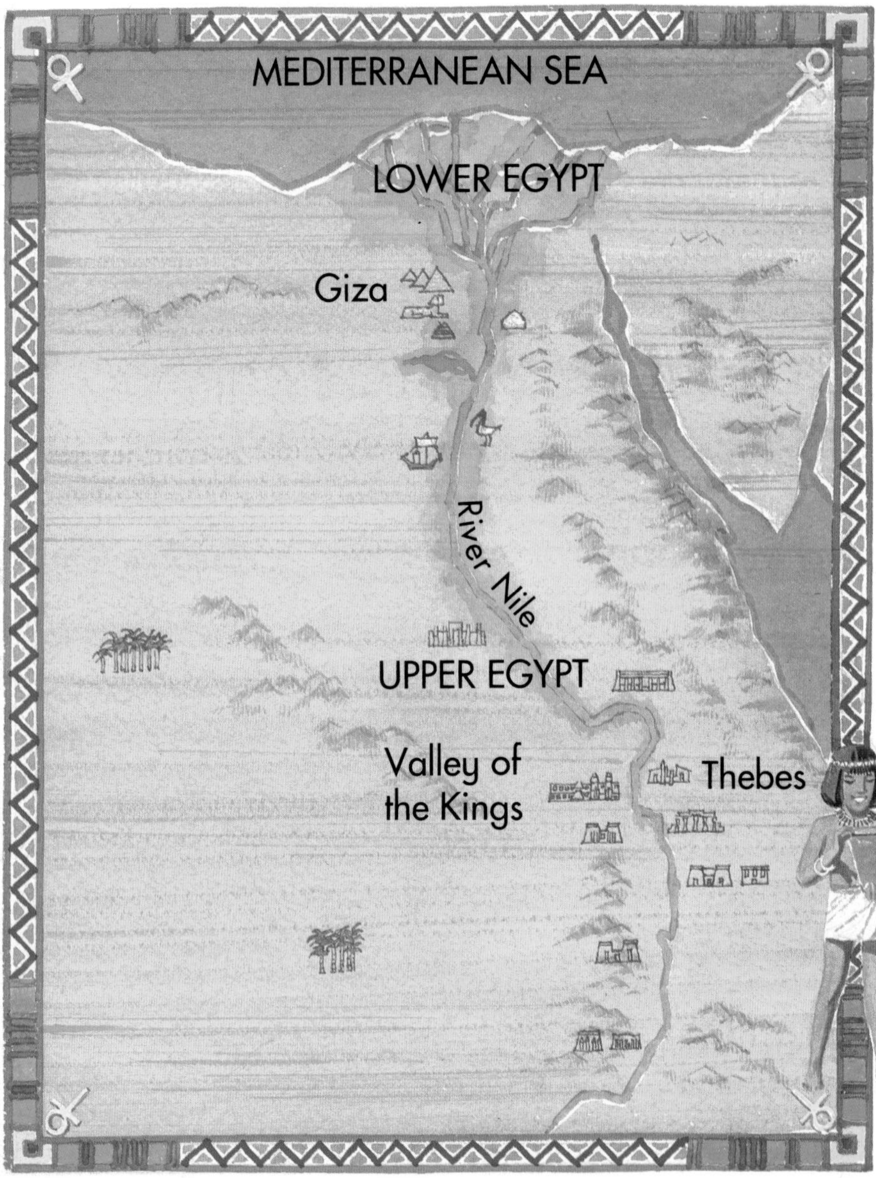

MEDITERRANEAN SEA

LOWER EGYPT

Giza

River Nile

UPPER EGYPT

Valley of the Kings

Thebes

Egypt is a long thin country and is mostly sand and rocks. The River Nile runs down the middle. People who came to Egypt had to live by the river because it was the only place where crops could grow.

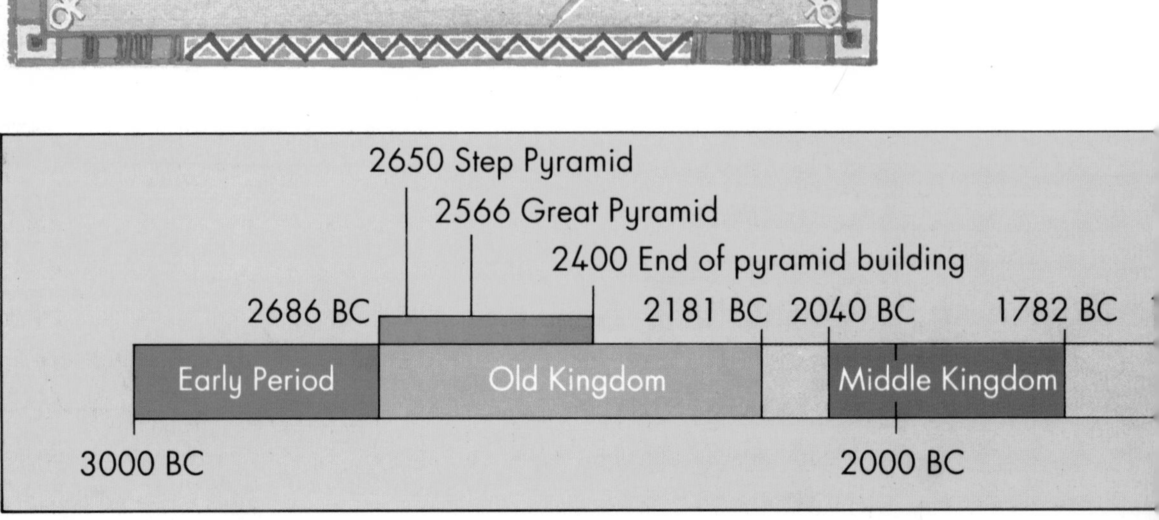

At first, the Egyptians lived in small groups. Later they formed two large groups. One group lived in Upper Egypt and the other lived in Lower Egypt. We say that the Ancient Egyptian civilization began when these two groups joined up. This civilization lasted a very long time. It started in about 3,000 BC, when the people of Upper and Lower Egypt started to work together. It ended in 30 BC, when the Romans took over. Sometimes there were wars, which caused a lot of confusion and starvation. The times of peace were called the Early Period, the Old Kingdom, the Middle Kingdom, the New Kingdom and the Late Period.

You can find these marked on the timeline below.

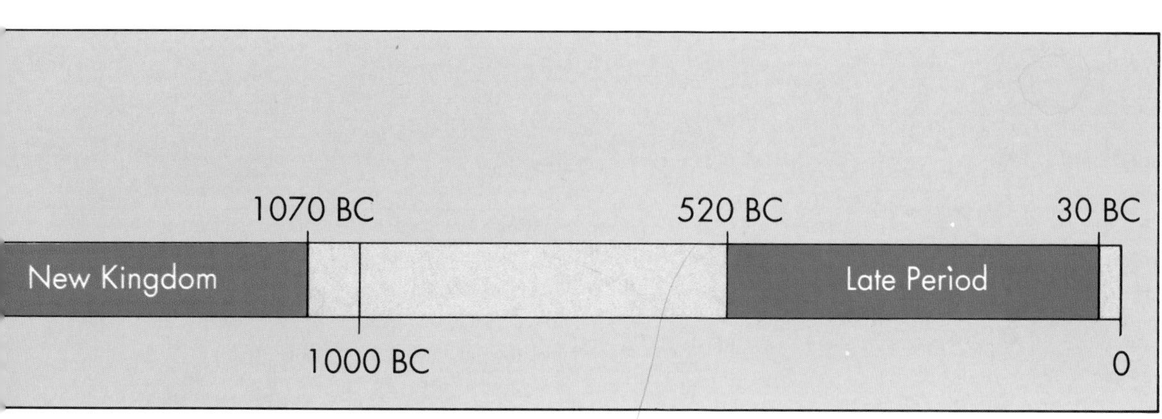

The River Nile

The River Nile floods every year. As the water goes down it leaves behind rich soil. The land which has been flooded is the only place where crops can grow.

People lived by the river because they could grow things there. The Egyptians wanted to grow more crops, but to do this they had to control the water. They had to stop some of the flood water from draining back into the river. They also had to find a way of getting water from the river all year. Controlling the water is called irrigation.

A shaduf. The Ancient Egyptians invented the shaduf to lift water from the River Nile. They are still used today.

The Egyptians got more than water from the Nile. Here we see a noble man hunting river birds to eat. The people also ate fish and used reeds to make baskets and boats.

The Egyptians saw that the flood water could be held back with ponds and canals. Then they could use the water. It was hard work to make the ponds and canals and they had to clear and repair them all the time. The Egyptians could only do this if they all worked together.

Farming

The Egyptians farmed the land when the flood waters of the River Nile went down. They had to grow crops that would be cut before the next flood. The most important crops were wheat and barley, which they used to make bread and beer. These were what most Egyptians ate and drank. Another important crop was flax, which was used to make cloth. The Egyptians grew fruit and vegetables, too. They ate a lot of onions and garlic, dates and grapes. Only rich people ate meat every day.

The Egyptians grew grapes to eat and to make wine.

Farmers and animals planting the seeds.

The Egyptians kept geese and cows to eat. They also hunted river birds and fish. The Egyptians had no farm machines so they used animals for some jobs. Goats and sheep trod the seed into the ground as soon as it was planted. An ox pulled the plough, and trampled the grain to get the husks off.

The pharaoh

The Egyptians had to work together to control the River Nile, and to farm it. People work together better if they have someone in charge. This helps to make sure that all the work is done at the right time. In Egypt this person was called the pharaoh. He was seen as more like a god than just a person. The Egyptians always had a pharaoh, unless they were fighting each other. When they fought there was no one to run the country, so people were fighting, not farming. Many died in the fighting. Those who were not killed were likely to starve because there was not enough food.

Pharaoh Tutankhamun's sarcophagus. He is holding signs for Upper and Lower Egypt. He has the goddesses of both parts on his crown. This is to show that he rules all of Egypt. *You can find out more about a sarcophagus on page 19.*

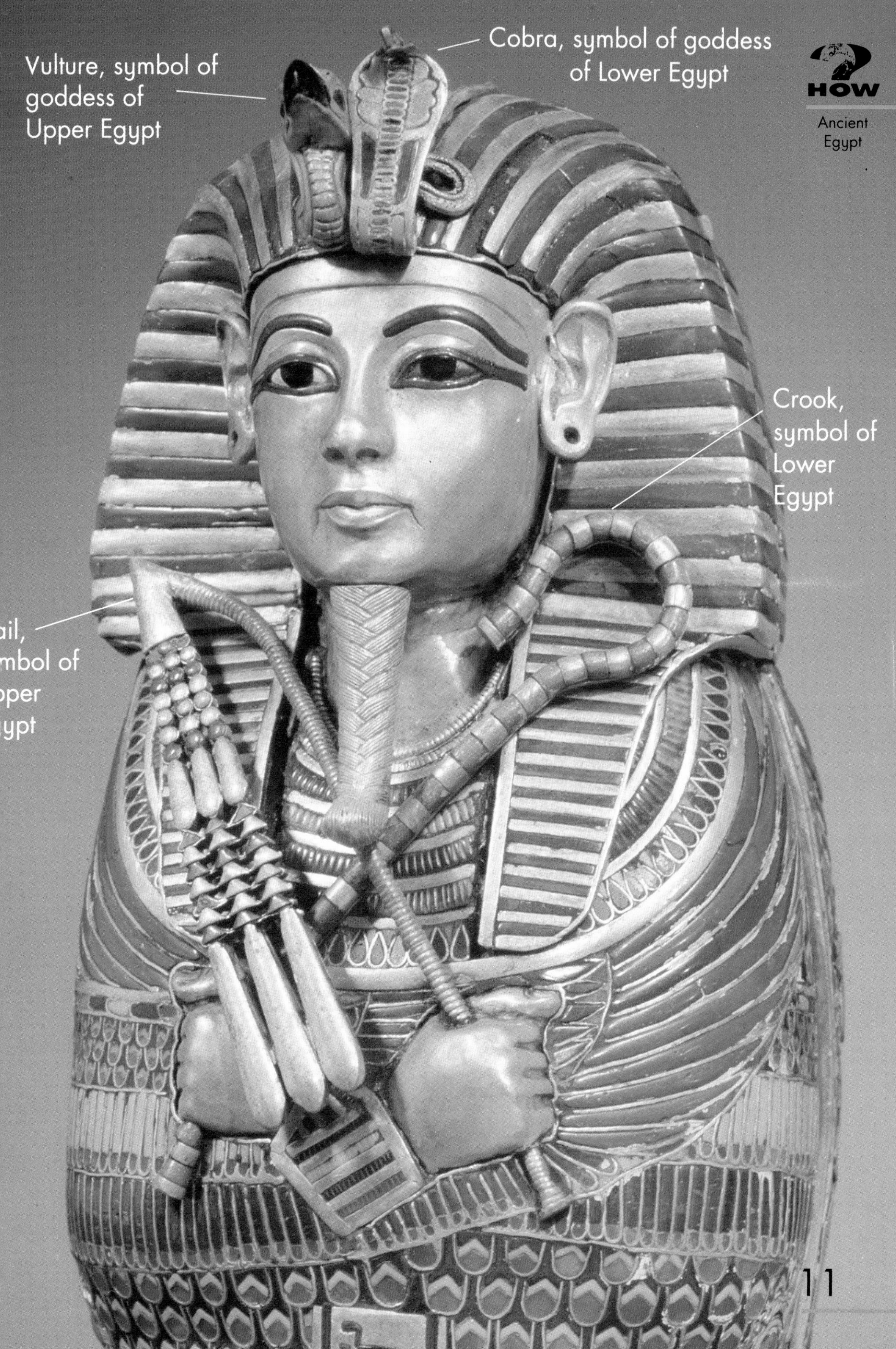
Vulture, symbol of goddess of Upper Egypt
Cobra, symbol of goddess of Lower Egypt
Crook, symbol of Lower Egypt
ail, mbol of pper ypt

How Egypt was ruled

The scribes were the only people who could write. This made them important because they could check all the food that was stored. Here a scribe is writing down how many geese there are.

On the next page is a picture to show how the Egyptians divided up the work. The pharaoh was at the top, giving out the work. Under him were the viziers, high priests and nobles. The Egyptians thought that all jobs were important except for the slaves, which were at the bottom. The Egyptians thought that their jobs were not very important.

Pharaoh Queen

Nobles

Grand Viziers of Upper and Lower Egypt

High Priest and
High Priestess

Governors

Craftsmen Artists

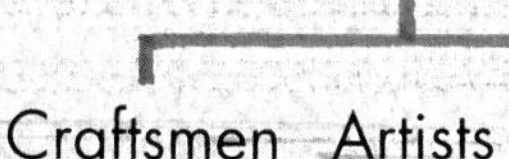

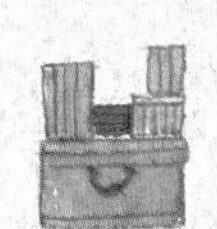

Scribes Tax Gatherers

Priests Priestesses

Builders Farmers

Scribes

Wab

Slaves

Trade

The Egyptians each did different jobs. Some were farmers and others were fishermen. Some made shoes, while some brewed beer and made bread. They did not have money to buy these things from each other, so they traded with each other to get the things that they wanted.

Markets were often by the river. They were where most trading was done.

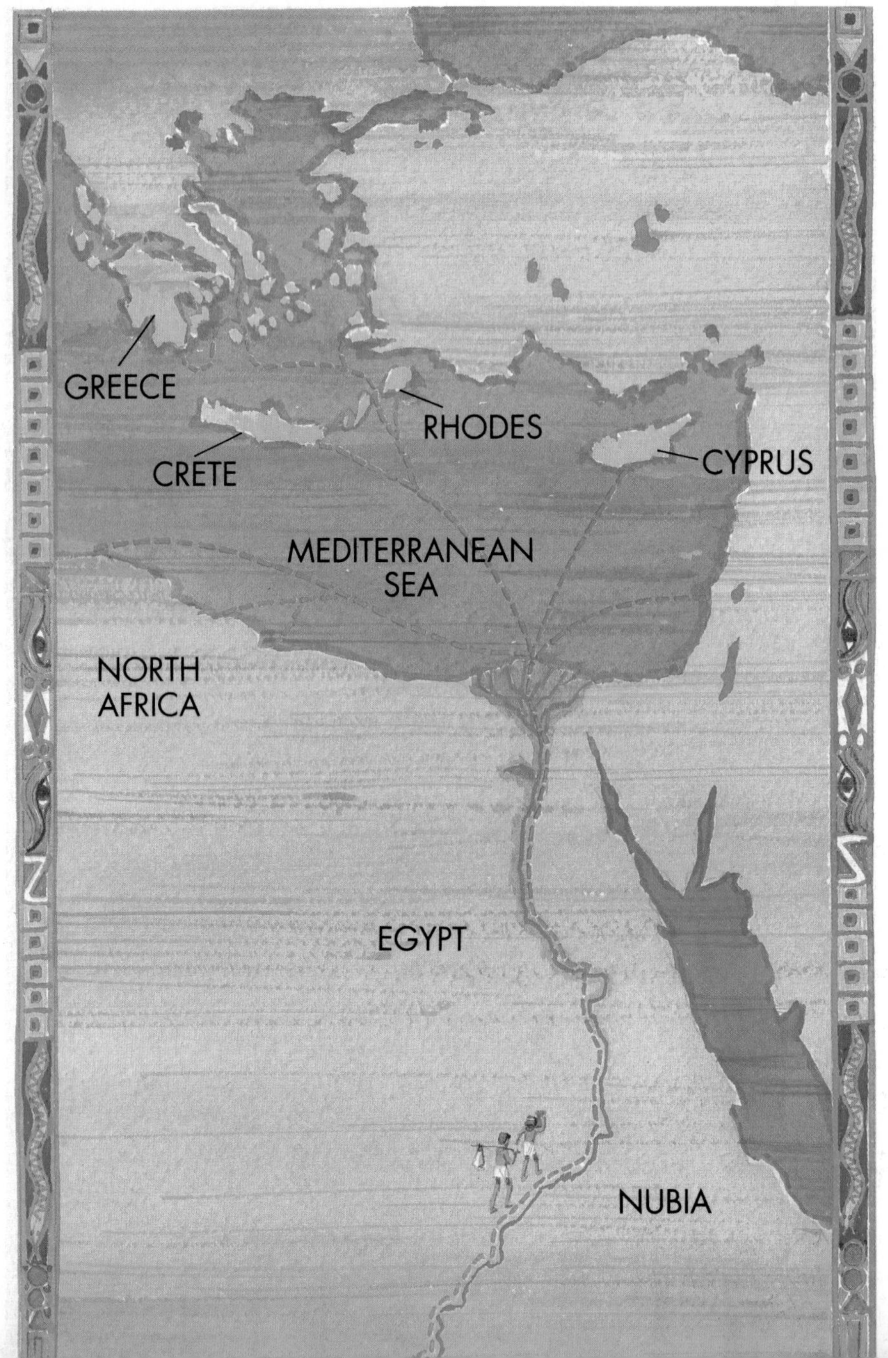

Places the Egyptians traded with.

The Egyptians also traded with other countries. They made more rope and flax than they needed. They often had more wheat than they would need in the coming year. They traded their extra supplies for things that they did not have, like wood, olive oil, silver and gold. They traded with other countries in the Mediterranean, mostly by boat.

Gods and goddesses

The Egyptians had lots of gods. Some of the gods were known by everyone. Other gods were only known by people in a certain area. The Egyptians saw important things, like the sun or the River Nile, as gods. They often drew gods with animal heads. Egyptians prayed to different gods at different times. If they thought that the River Nile was not going to flood, they prayed to the river goddess, Hapi. If a child was ill, Hapi was no help. Then they prayed to Bes, god of children, or Imhotep, god of medicine.

The Egyptians saw gods all around them, all the time. They wanted to pray often, so each house had a shrine. This was a place to pray at any time. They built big temples, which they used on special days.

The gods judge a dead man. They balance his heart against the feather of truth. If he has been good he can go to the Fields of Iaru (Heaven). If he has been bad, Ammut eats him.

Hunefer

Osiris

Mummies

The Egyptians thought that a person who died went to a new world. They would need their body in this world, so they had to stop it from going bad. First they cut out the soft insides. They put these in jars to be placed with the mummy. Then they hooked the brain out through the nose. They rubbed oils on the body. They put four or five layers of cloth around it, like bandages.

These Egyptian priests are oiling and wrapping a body.

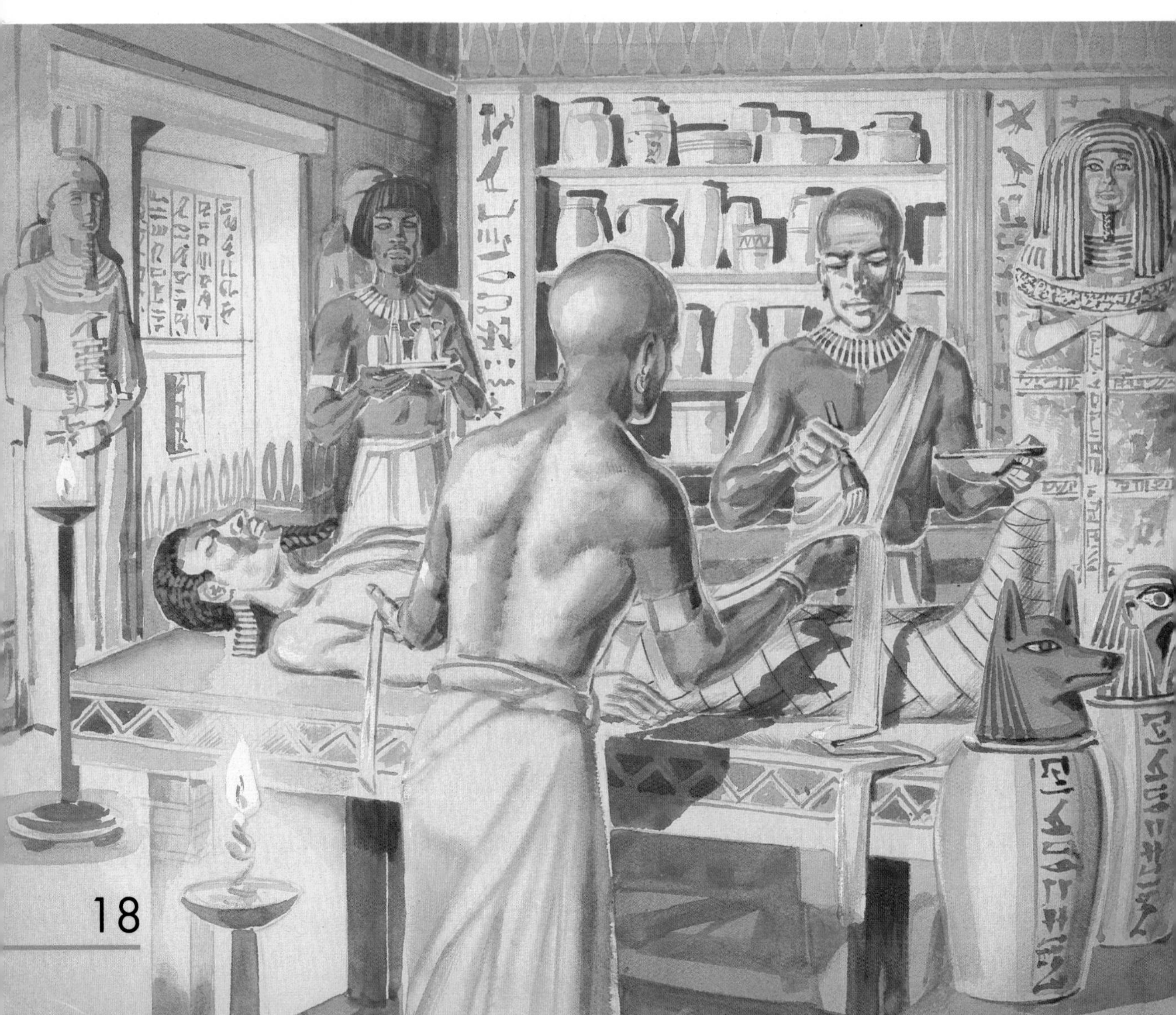

A priestess in her sarcophagus. It shows what she looked like.

They sometimes gave the mummy a face mask. It looked like the person in real life. A rich person would have their jewels put on it. The mummy was put in a painted case called a sarcophagus. They buried the mummies in the ground or put them in tombs. Only some of the first pharaohs had pyramids. Most of them were buried in tombs cut in the rock in the Valley of Kings.

Pyramids

Only the pharaohs were buried in pyramids. Pyramids were built out of big stone blocks. The blocks had to be dug up and cut to size. Then they had to be moved to the right place by sliding them along on wooden rollers. It took lots of men a long time to build a pyramid.

The stone blocks had to be dragged up ramps which got higher and higher. They had no cranes or even wheels.

The Great Pyramid. It took 5,000 men 20 years to build. It is made from over 2,300,000 blocks of stone.

The mummy of the dead pharaoh was put into a small room in the middle of the pyramid. He had lots of things he might need for his next life. There were jewels, food, furniture, pots, and even model dolls to work for him. The entrances were closed up, but the pyramids were often robbed, so the workers made secret rooms to bury the pharaohs in, with traps to catch the thieves.

Everyday life

Egyptian life had a pattern. All the women worked in the home. Most Egyptian men worked at two jobs. When the water in the Nile was low they worked on the land. Only the most important people and the priests did not farm the land. When the Nile flooded, the farmers had other jobs. Some were builders or fishermen. Others were artists or jewellers.

Egyptians had very little furniture.

It was very hot in Egypt, so people did not wear many clothes. Men, women and children wore either thin cloth kilts or robes. Women wore as much make-up and jewels as they could afford to. People shaved off all their hair, to keep cooler. They had wigs to wear on special occasions.

Egyptian clothes looked very like this. The big lumps on the ladies' heads are scented lumps of fat. They melted in the heat and ran down their faces to keep them cool and make them smell nice.

Houses

The Egyptians built all houses in the same way. The houses of important people had more rooms. They had lovely painted walls inside, but they looked the same on the outside. They used mud bricks for building. The walls were thick, to keep out the heat. Because it did not rain very often, there was no need to have sloping roofs to carry the rain away. The flat roofs were part of the house. People sat on their roofs, or dried washing there. Most people cooked outside, so if they had no yard they did their cooking on the roof too. The houses had rooms under the ground. These rooms were dark and cool. They were very good for storing food and drink.

Inside an Egyptian craftsman's house.

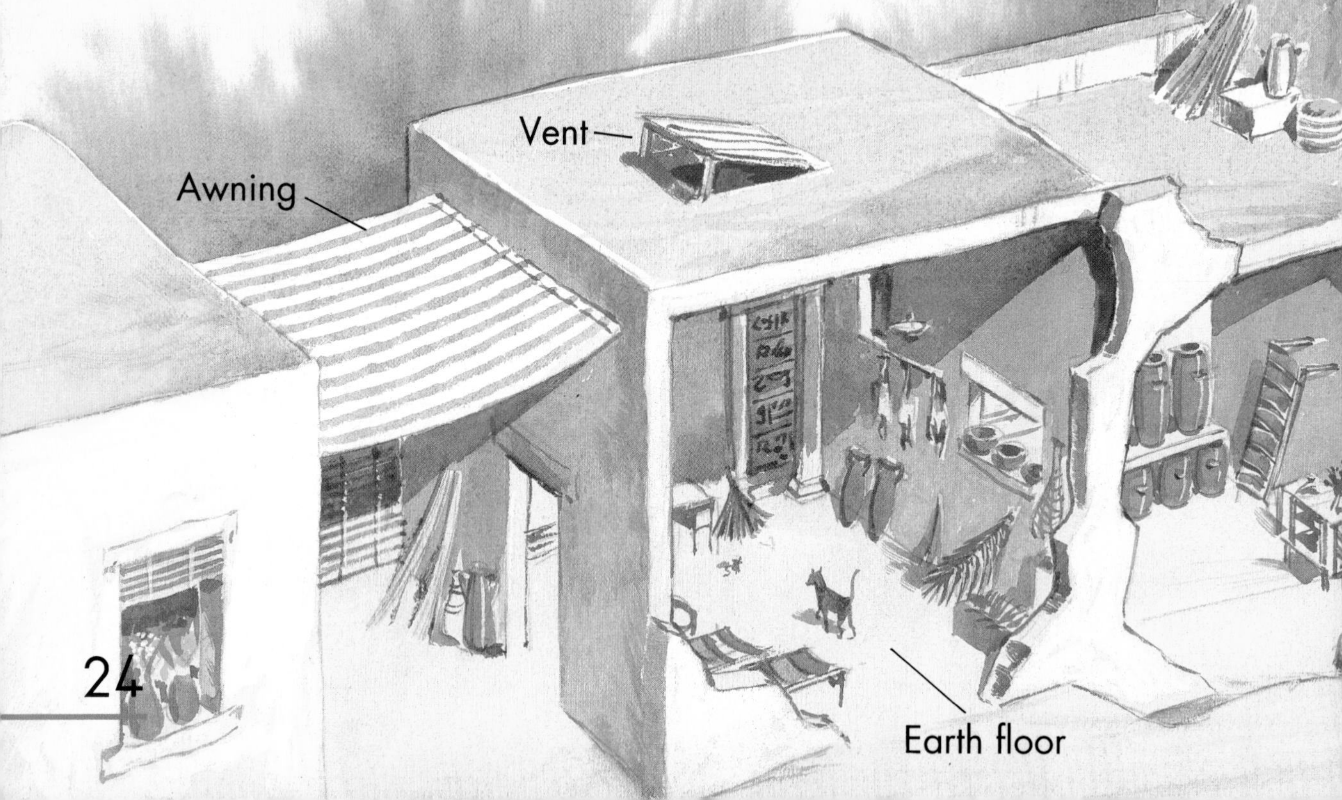

32610.

Model of an Egyptian house.

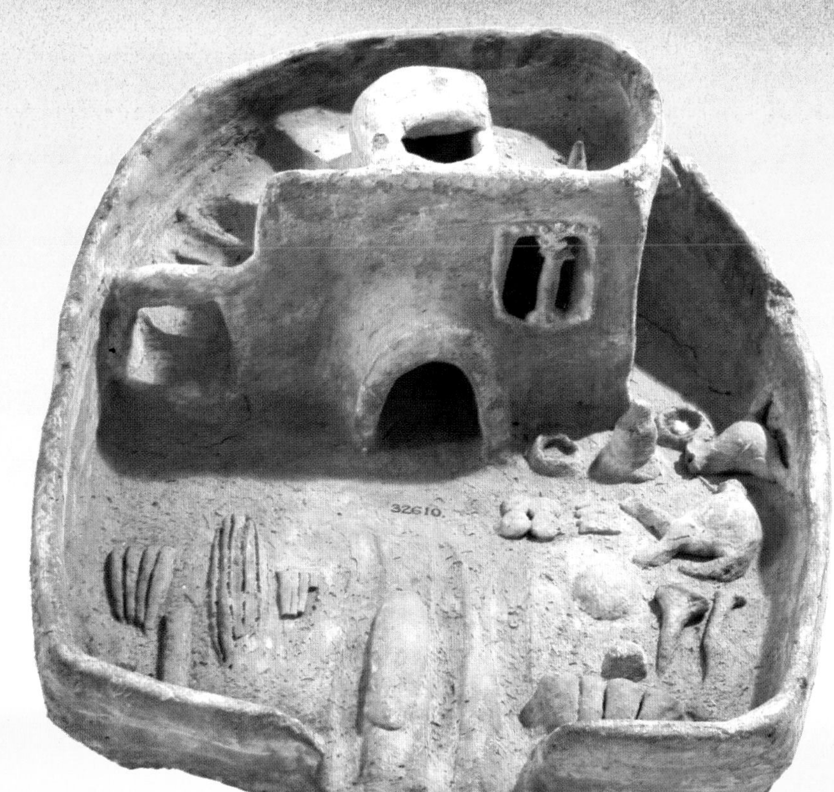

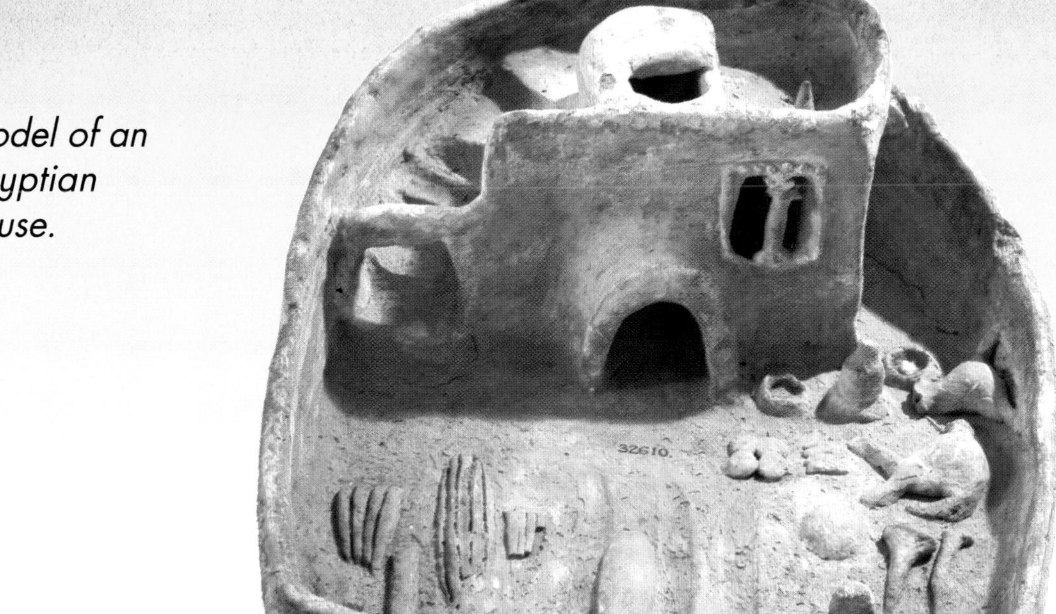

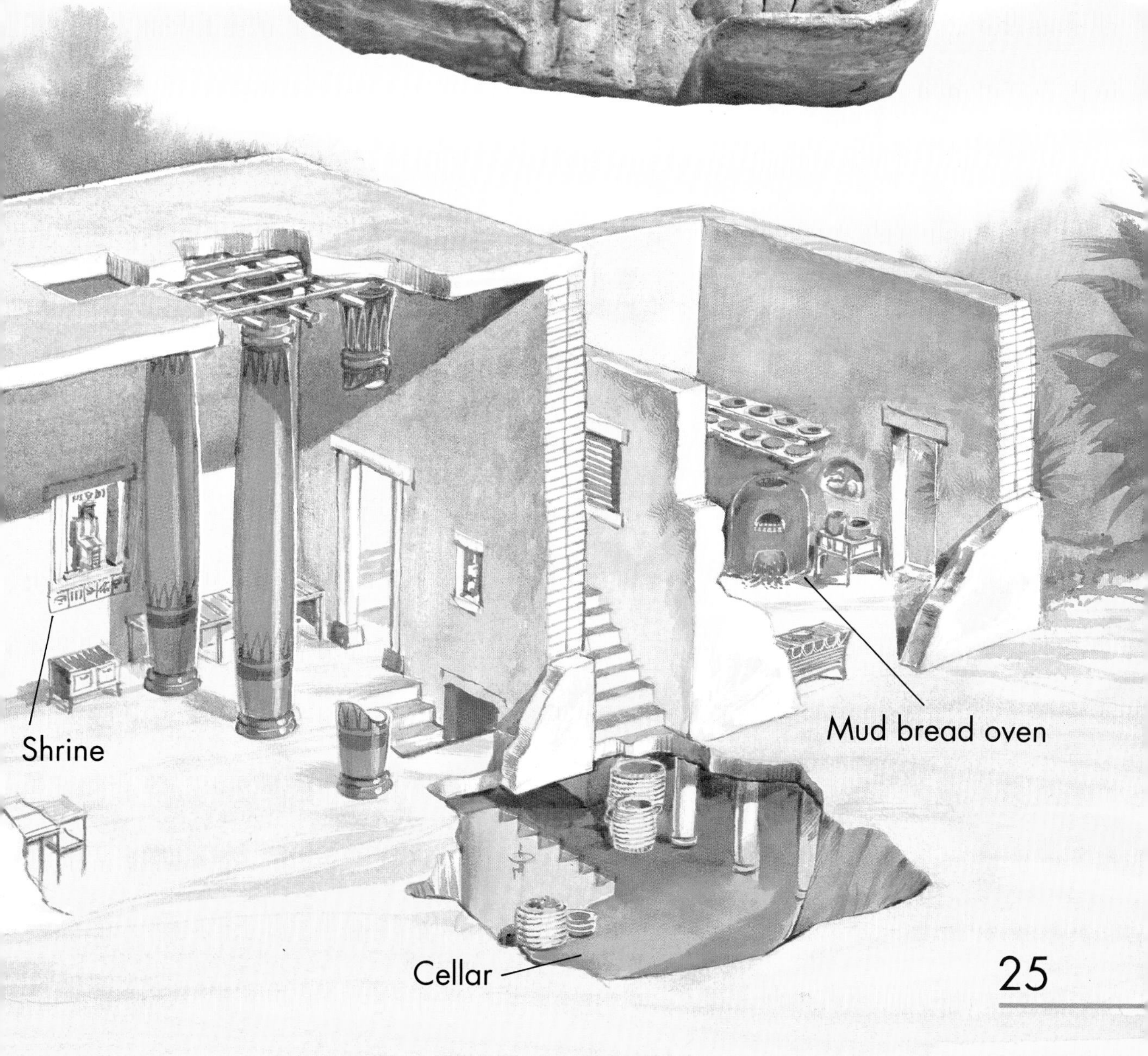
Shrine
Mud bread oven
Cellar

Children

Children at work.

Children in Egypt grew up to do the same job as their parents. Girls stayed at home with their mothers. They learned how to look after the house, bake bread and weave flax. Boys went to work with their fathers, and helped as much as they could. They only went to school if they were going to work as a scribe.

Very young children stayed at home with their mothers. Many of their games were like games children play today. They played racing, tag and leap frog. They had balls and wooden toys. Older children played a game like chess, called senet.

Some children's toys. They are made from wood and reeds.

Medicine

The Egyptians tried to make people well in different ways. They made medicines from plants. They tried to keep clean. Rich Egyptians washed at least twice a day. Everyone tried to wash clothes and dishes often. Making mummies helped them to find out more about how the body worked. They saw the lungs, heart, liver and stomach of a person when they took them out of the body to stop it rotting. This helped them to think of better cures.

An Egyptian doctor's tools.

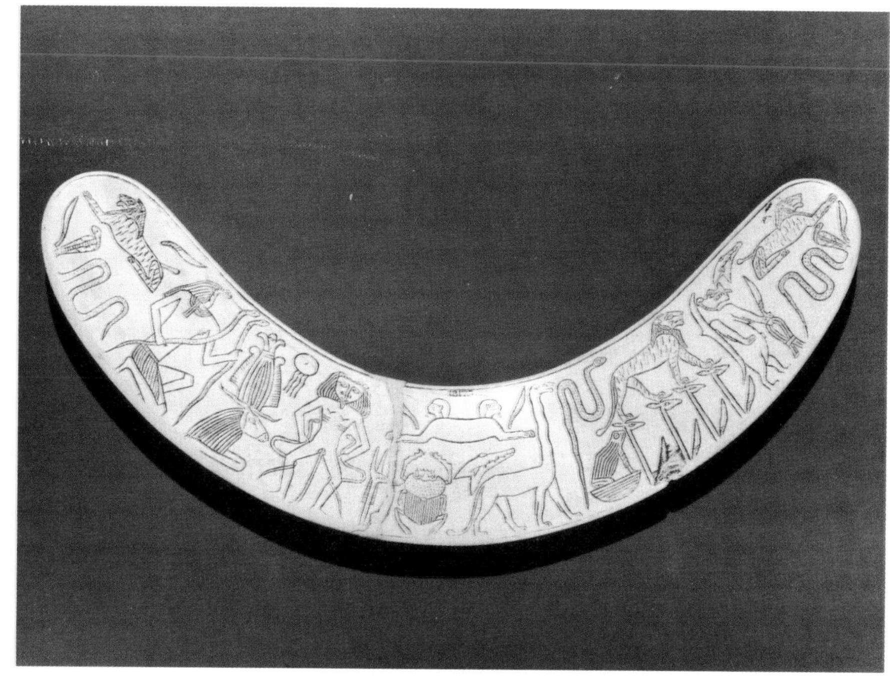

An ivory charm to keep people safe when they were asleep. It has pictures of gods, and knives to cut wild animals.

The Egyptians also believed in magic. They thought that evil spirits made people ill, and prayed to a god to make the spirits go away. They drank magic drinks to make them well, and wore magic charms to keep evil spirits away.

A magic potion recipe. It has beetles and a snake's head in it.

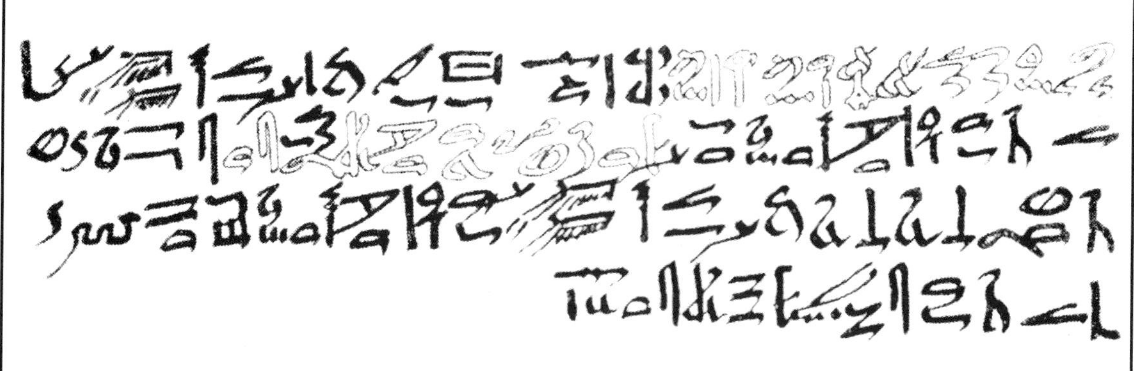

Tutankhamun

Tutankhamun is the most famous of the pharaohs. He was only about eight years old when he became pharaoh. He did not live long enough to fight in a battle and become famous. He did not rule for long enough to be seen as a wise ruler. He is famous just because his people hid his tomb so well that it is the only tomb of a pharaoh that has not been robbed. It was hidden under the tomb of another pharaoh.

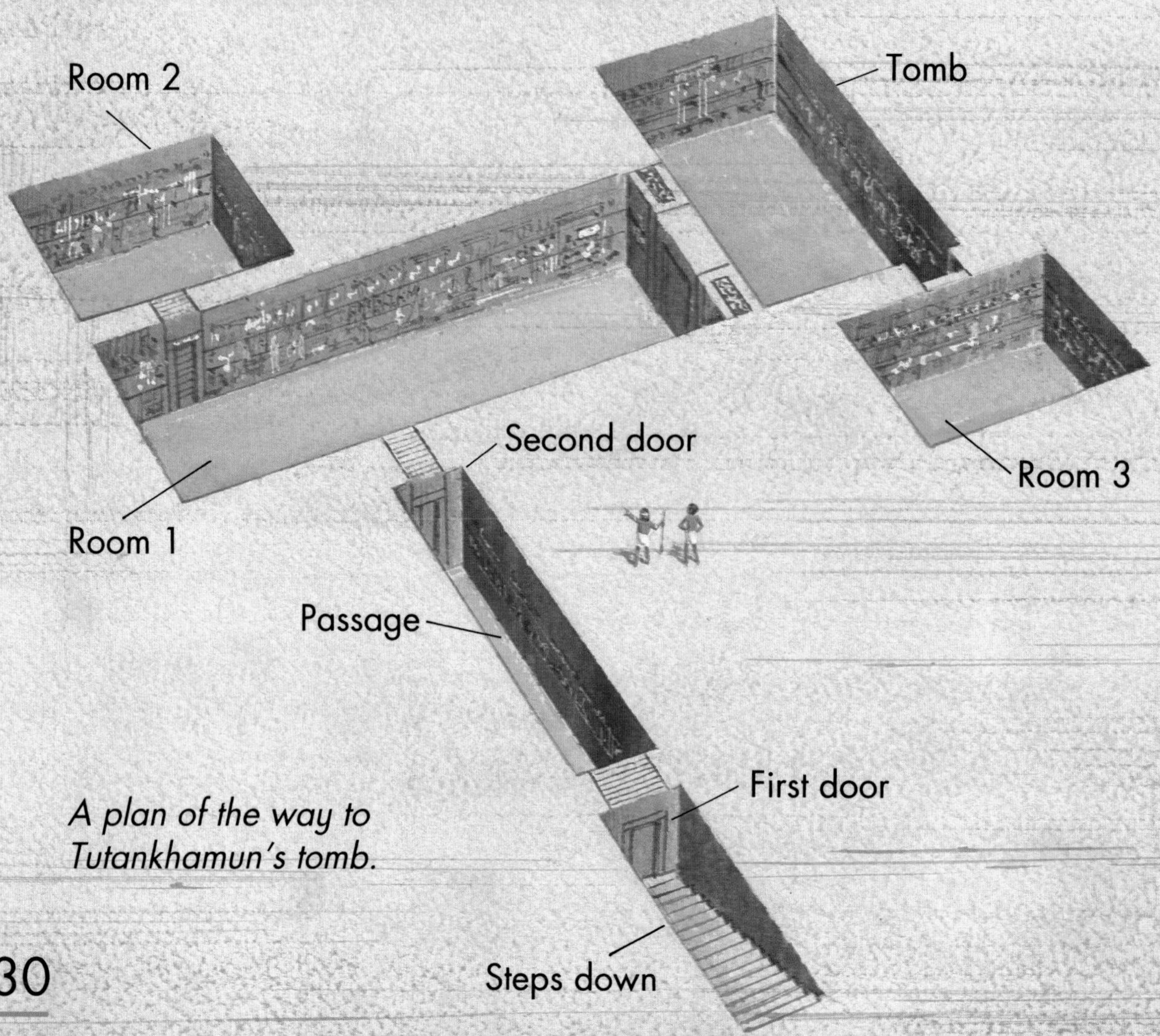

A plan of the way to Tutankhamun's tomb.

Just some of the many 'wonderful things' that Carter found.

Tutankhamun's tomb was found in 1922. The tomb had several rooms, all full of treasure. When they made a hole in the wall of the first room, the archaeologist Howard Carter looked in. They asked what he could see. He said 'Wonderful things'.

Index

ANCIENT CIVILIZATIONS

The Ancient Egyptians

JANE SHUTER

Acknowledgements
The author and publishers are grateful to the following for permission to reproduce copyright photographs:
British Museum, pp. 7, 8,12,16/17, 19, 22, 25, 27, 29 (top), 31; Robert Harding Picture Library, p.12; Michael Holford, p. 21; Wellcome Institute Library, p. 28; Hulton Picture Company, p. 29 (bottom).

92 93 94 95 9 8 7 6 5 4 3

Designed by Miller, Craig and Cocking.

Illustrated by Tony Maguire

Printed in Spain
by Mateu Cromo Artes Graficas SA

Heinemann Educational,
a division of Heinemann Educational Books Ltd,
Halley Court, Jordan Hill, Oxford OX2 8EJ

OXFORD LONDON EDINBURGH
MADRID ATHENS BOLOGNA PARIS
MELBOURNE SYDNEY AUCKLAND SINGAPORE TOKYO
IBADAN NAIROBI HARARE GABORONE
PORTSMOUTH NH (USA)

0 435 04206 8 softback
0 435 04361 7 hardback